The Fit Is IT!!

How Custom Club Fitting Matters To YOUR Golfing Dreams

Tony Wright

The Fit Is IT!!

Copyright © 2013 by Tony Wright

To my wife Diane…

Who never wavered in supporting me in developing my club fitting passion, even when I would come home from my 35-year day job and spend 2 or 3 hours at night building golf clubs.
Crazy woman – lucky man!
187 plus months of marital bliss.

Thank you!

Acknowledgments

To the Lord – who never ceases to provide me with exactly what I need when I need it.

To Nick Londino, Dick Swanson, Marshall Brown, and Duncan Brown – Who ensured that I was able to attend Carnegie-Mellon University on a Western PGA Caddy Scholarship, and who simply always cared about and encouraged me.

To Richard Hess, now deceased – For opening my eyes to the value of custom club fitting, helping me play better golf, and for the initial inspiration to become a club fitter.

To Roy Nix – Founder of the AGCP – and to all of my AGCP friends – For helping and guiding me to become a better club fitter, and for your friendships.

To Tom Wishon, Tom Wishon Golf – You are a continued inspiration to all of us club fitters, and how you take the time to personally respond to email questions, usually within a day, is beyond me. I think it is because you continue to have a PASSION about club fitting!

To Bobby Dean and Edel Golf (www.edelgolf.com) – Thanks for teaching me so much about putter and wedge fitting!

To Glen Coombe, "The Putting Doctor" (www.puttingdoctor.net) – Thanks for training me to use the SAM PuttLab, and for continuing almost every day to teach me something new to help golfers improve their putting strokes!

To Des Mahoney, PGA Teaching Professional (www.desmahoneygolf.com) – Thanks for allowing me to find a home for my club fitting work at the Centennial Golf Academy about 4 years ago, and for your continued friendship and support.

To Ray Perry of MarketBlazer – For you guidance on "all things marketing" in the last 2 years, and for always being available to talk to with a question or request for help.

To Sue LaPointe from Triumph Communications – Who made my engineer-writing into something that people could read, and who kept encouraging me to write this book.

To all of my Golfing Buddies – Who I think wonder sometimes why I do this instead of playing more golf, but who love me anyhow!

And to my wife Diane – I love you, you are a saint!

Foreword

Tony Wright is an AGCP member and good friend. Tony recently sent me a book he wrote to read and offer my opinions on. Tony has been a member of the AGCP from almost the beginning of the organization. He was a fellow PCS member before the PCS dissolved and joined the AGCP almost immediately once it was opened up to membership. Over the years Tony has had an insatiable appetite for knowledge and he was in the beginning, and is today, very passionate about all he does. It seems there has hardly been a week gone by that I haven't received an email from Tony asking a question about fitting or how to market his clubfitting business.

Although when Tony sent his book I was in the middle of building an addition to my fitting studio, I found myself going back to Tony's book as often as I had time to sit down and read. I wanted to find out all the nuggets Tony has buried in the pages of his book. Although by most accounts I am very versed in clubfitting it is always interesting to get more information from a fellow clubfitter to broaden my perspective and I always learn new things no matter who I read. Tony did not disappoint. Not only was it informative I think it is written so that anyone can understand the meaning behind the words that will encourage them to "Get Fit" as soon as possible. Even though I have been a golf professional for over 40 years and as an AGCP Master Fitter and a Golf Digest selection as one of America's Best 100 Clubfitters I found a number of helpful ideas in Tony's book.

If you are a golfer and you want to improve your golf game dramatically and you are looking for a solution, then you came to the right (tempted to say Wright) place to educate yourself. Tony tells you in terms you can understand all about the nuts and bolts of why custom clubfitting benefits all golfers, not just the very good golfers. Tony describes how and why putter fitting, driver fitting, iron fitting and wedge fitting will help you or any golfer not only lower your scores but enjoy the game more.

If you want to hit more solid shots more often, if you want to hit consistently longer and straighter shots, if you want to hit more tee shots in the fairway, if you want to hit iron shots closer to the pin consistently and have more makeable birdie putts, if you want to make more of those birdies and 3 putt less often on those longer putts... You need to read this book.

Tony related to me recently how he used one of my favorite techniques to help a golfer who had a tendency to duck hook a tee shot now and then by adding weight to his driver head to delay the face closing at impact. The golfer's big sweeping draw became a gentle draw and the duck hooks went away. Tony cites a number of real world solutions that illustrate why a custom clubfitter is the best possible way to improve your golf game.

As the director of the AGCP, as a Master Clubfitter, as a Golf Digest selection as one of America's Best 100 club-fitters, and as a good friend, essentially on every level imaginable I delight in seeing Tony writing a book about clubfitting. His knowledge and ability have come from curious to expert over the years and I've marveled in his growth from part-time to full-time and the passion he brings to his efforts to help golfers of all abilities.

Roy Nix
McNix Golf
Midland, GA
www.McNixGolf.com
762-821-3148
r.nix@McNixGolf.com
Assoc. of Golf Clubfitting Professionals
www.agcpgolf.com
706-507-0095

Table of Contents

Why – Really!
You Should Read this Book

Ray Perry, my marketing guru and great friend, said to me "Why don't you write a book containing some of your past blog posts and newsletters?" Sounds easy enough in principle – review 4 years of materials and find information of most value to golfers, assemble together, get great copywriting help, a good cover and presto – a book!

Not so fast though. The idea of doing so seemed good; many of the old posts would hopefully be of value to golfers. But it still nagged at me – really why do this?

Well, on the evening of November 28, 2012 I had one of those "Ask and You Shall Receive" moments (another topic for another time!) and realized the why.

The purpose of this book is to light a spark within a golfer who does not really understand what True Custom Club Fitting is. There is a group of True Club Fitters out there who have an absolute Passion to help golfers play to their potential. And the sad truth is that many, many golfers keep buying new clubs ever year or two hoping to find magic –

based on the millions of dollars that the golfing industry spends on marketing one-size-fits-all golf clubs.

The truth though – like many truths in the world, often hidden from most – is that True Custom Club Fitters can create this magic. They do it by one-one-one personal interactions with golfers. They create and build golf clubs that are unique for each individual golfer. And when they create this magic – they are as giddy as the golfer is about the results!

So thank you for reading this book. I hope it gives you some glimpses into the world of Custom Club Fitting – and lights a spark in you to find out more. Not primarily because someone like me will make money from you doing so – but because it is a lot more fun to play the golf of your dreams!

Please be kind and leave a review for this book on Amazon.com. Your feedback will help me improve the next version. Thanks!

The Story of My Custom Club Fitting Passion

About a dozen years ago, I bought a new driver – an OEM driver, 7 degrees of loft. I was "custom fitted" for that driver at a demo on a driving range. After playing with the driver for a period of time, I wanted to find out why I could not hit it well.

I was aware of a custom club fitter in Oak Ridge – Richard Hess. At that time Richard worked at the Centennial Golf Course – so I paid him a visit. He took my driver, measured the shaft flex of it (it was supposed to be S flex) and said it was WAY stiffer than that – in fact said it had the flex of a board! Red faced and steaming, I asked if he could build me a driver – which he did, a great one that I played for a number of years. He also fit me for a set of irons and these also were the best I had ever played with.

I continued to visit Richard from time to time, and during one of my visits saw a book on his shelf titled "The Search for the Perfect Golf Club," by Tom Wishon. I bought it, read it, and became hooked.

In late 2005 and 2006, I started to think about what I would do after I retired from my career at the Oak Ridge National Laboratory (ORNL). One morning in June 2006, I woke up and a thought came to me "learn to become a custom golf club fitter." Well, I know enough to trust thoughts like these. Right around that time I got a $300 gift card for 30 years of service at ORNL. I spent all of that money on a package set of golf clubs to build and some starting shop club making materials. That led to attending a week-long club making class at Golfworks in October 2006, to joining the Professional Clubmakers Society and attending an annual conference in the spring of 2007, and to joining the Association of Golf Clubfitting Professionals (AGCP) in 2008 and attending my first AGCP Roundtable training event in the fall of 2008.

Each and every day since that "little voice" talked to me in June 2006, I have loved learning the art and science of club fitting and club making, and using that knowledge to help golfers play better golf.

The Basics Of "The Fit Is IT"

If Tiger Says It, It MUST Be True!

The note below was in the November 2009 Golf Digest magazine.

ASK TIGER — Golf Digest, Nov'09, p.280.

Q. What is the best tip you would give to a beginner? (Anne Patterson, Boulder, CO)

A. "Find clubs that fit you. It will save you a ton of aggravation from the start. Make sure they aren't too short, long or heavy. Otherwise, you'll adapt your swing to the equipment in a way that might not be technically sound. It's easy to get fit, and it really does matter."

Probably cannot say this any better than this......thanks Tiger!

21 – "Plus 2" – Custom Club Fitting Variables

The Association of Golf Clubfitting Professionals (AGCP) has published a list of 21 major variables that affect golf club performance and that can be part of a true custom club fitting. These variables are:

1. Clubhead loft
2. Clubhead lie angle
3. Clubhead bulge (woods only)
4. Clubhead roll (woods only)
5. Club head sole angle (irons only)
6. Clubhead face angle (woods only)
7. Clubhead hosel offset
8. Clubhead material and design
9. Shaft flex
10. Shaft torque
11. Shaft weight
12. Shaft spine alignment
13. Shaft flex profile
14. Shaft material composition and design
15. Grip size
16. Grip weight
17. Grip material composition and design
18. Club length
19. Club swingweight / moment of inertia
20. Club total weight

21. Club set makeup

In almost every true custom club fitting, at least 10 of these variables are involved.

However, there are two additional variables that are also of critical importance to a successful true custom club fitting. These are: a) as Keith Chatham (an AGCP Master Club Fitter) reminded me recently – golf club feel; and b) an evaluation of the golf swing of the golfer, to determine if swing changes are needed or how some of the major club fitting variables can be used to improve performance without swing changes.

Russ Ryden, a Golf Digest Top 100 club fitter, coined a new term – Consumer Clubs. To me, consumer clubs are clubs that you buy in a store without any fitting that are made for the "masses", or clubs where you get a minimal level of fitting. What do you think – do you deserve consumer clubs?

Golf Shaftology 101: Some Basics for Iron Shafts

Golf shafts are clearly an important part of every golf club. Some say they are the "engine of the golf club" and some do not agree - but finding the right shaft(s) for your woods and irons will improve the consistency of your shots and - if you were playing a shaft that did not fit you - how far you can hit your clubs. Here are some of the basics for iron shafts:

Iron shafts. There are four basic categories of shafts for irons - including wedges - that you should be aware of:

<u>Taper tip iron shafts</u>
Taper tip iron shafts are the ones that you typically find in OEM clubs that you purchase in golf stores. At the tip end of the shaft - where the shaft goes into the iron hosel - the diameter is 0.355 inches and it increases to approx. 0.370 inches at the end of the hosel. Many of the PGA professionals like to play taper tip shafts because they are "constant weight" shafts - the shaft weight for each iron is approximately the same. They come in different "flexes" – A, R, S, X as examples - and the exact flexes of the shafts cannot, for most taper tip shafts, be adjusted significantly.

Parallel tip iron shafts

Parallel tip iron shafts started to be available in the 1970s, largely due to manufacturer's desire to control inventories of shafts. As the name implies, parallel tip shafts have a tip end that is a constant diameter - in this case 0.370 inches. Many club fitters prefer to use parallel tip shafts because they can tip the end of the shafts to achieve a specific shaft flex throughout an iron set, based on the best fit for a player. Parallel tip shafts are not constant weight shafts, so the shaft weight goes down as you move from longer to shorter irons.

Shaft material - steel or graphite

For the most part most PGA tour players play steel shafts. However, there are a wide range of excellent graphite and steel shafts available to help us "mere mortals" achieve good results. Graphite shafts are available in different flexes and weights from around 50 grams up to 120 to 130 grams raw weight. For a long time steel shafts were only available from about 100 to 130 grams, but now there are steel shafts available down to about 75 grams raw weight. There is a myth that graphite shafts are not high quality, this is simply not true.

Specialty shafts

There are iron shafts available specifically for use in wedges (sometimes called "spinner" shafts to promote lower ball flight and high spin rates) and also shafts designed specifically for hybrid clubs. Both of these types of specialty shafts are available in steel or graphite.

Golf Shaftology 102: Some Basics for Wood Shafts

The shafts that are used in drivers and fairway woods, in most cases these days, are graphite shafts. They have a number of characteristics that affect how they perform for different players of different strengths and skill levels. Some of the most important characteristics that can be varied include these:

Shaft "flex"
When companies talk about shaft flex, they are typically talking about the flex of the shaft measured at the end of the club - the "butt flex." This is what R, S, X flexes mean on a shaft. And as many of you know, there is no standard for what a specific butt flex is for a shaft. Most people purchase a driver in a store based on the shaft butt flex.

Shaft "flex profile"
The flex of a graphite or steel shaft is not constant across the length of the shaft - if you measure flex 45 inches from the head of the club and 15 inches from the end of the club you will most likely get different flexes. A shaft that is "butt stiff" and "tip stiff" may work well for a player; but that same player may have difficulty hitting a driver that has a shaft that is "butt stiff" and "tip soft." Many professional clubfitters work to find a shaft for a player with the right

flex profile to match how they swing their driver and fairway woods.

Shaft weight

There are a wide range of shaft weights available for use in drivers and fairway woods. The typical weight range is from about 50 grams to 100 grams uncut weight for graphite shafts – and lighter shafts in the range of 40 weight are being developed. The shaft weight has a large influence on the total weight of a driver or fairway wood - and on the golfers swing path with these clubs. Some players actually can get better performance with steel shafts in their drivers; these can weigh in the range of 100 to 130 grams.

Most of the quality driver and fairway wood shafts that can be purchased have 0.335 inch tip diameters, and custom build drivers and fairway woods have hosels that use these tip diameters. A little known fact is that many of the OEM drivers available use 0.350 tip diameter shafts - largely to reduce the possibility that these shafts will break at the tip. The drivers that the PGA tour players use typically are not the same as you can buy in stores - they have hosels designed for 0.335 inch tip diameters.

Club Weight Feel - Swingweight vs. MOI?

Many, if not all of you, are familiar with the term "swingweight" as a measure of how heavy golf clubs feel, and how this weight feel affects the performance of golf clubs. It has been an important golf club fitting parameter for many years. There is growing evidence, however, that there may be a better way to build clubs so that the weight feel is truly optimized for players - MOI, or Moment of Inertia matching. As discussed below, MOI Matching is old and new.

Much of the information in this section comes from a note from the Dave Tutleman website: (http://www.tutelman.com/golf/design/swingwt1.php), and also from information from Richard Kempton, an experienced club fitter in the United Kingdom (http://www.theclubdoctors.co.uk/moi_matching.html).

First though – why does swingweight or MOI of a golf club matter? Well, for two reasons. First, the higher the swingweight or MOI of a golf club, the more difficult it can be to close the face of the club at impact. Second, golf club swingweight or MOI affects the overall feel of a golf club and how a player can feel or not feel the club head as he swings it.

In the early 1900s, clubmakers building clubs for
professionals by matching clubs based on the product of
the head weight and the square of the length of the golf
club. So the longer the clubs would be, the lighter the
heads would have to be for the clubs to be "matched."
Clubmakers at that time found that matching clubs this way
took a lot of calculations and time.

In 1930 Robert Adams, a clubmaker, invented the
swingweight scale. It is a balance between the head weight
end of a club versus the grip weight end of the club, using a
14 inch pivot from the grip end of the club. Around 1945
Kenneth Smith bought Adam's rights to the swingweight
scale. The most often used version of the scale uses a 14
inch fulcrum. Adams developed a letter scale for measures
of swingweight. Higher letters relate to higher swingweights,
and higher numbers within a letter group relate to higher
swingweights. Men's clubs purchased in stores often have
swingweights in the range of D-1, while women's clubs
purchased in stores often have swingweights in the range of
C-6.

In terms of swingweight higher head weights, higher shaft
weights, and lower grip weights lead to higher values of
swingweight. So, for example, you could have a club that
has a D-1 swingweight, add 4 grams of weight to the head
and 10 grams of weight to the grip end, and it would still be

a D-1. Swingweight is a static measurement of the weight feel of a golf club.

Within the last 10 to 15 years, another method of measuring the weight feel of a golf club has been used primarily by custom clubfitters. This method is MOI (moment of inertia) matching. The MOI of a golf club is a measurement of how much force it takes to put the club into motion around the grip end of the club. It has units of mass times length squared - interestingly, the same units clubmakers used in the early 1900s for their club matching! Now, though, there are devices available that can easily and quickly measure the MOI of golf clubs.

MOI is a measure of the dynamic feel of a golf club, while swingweight is a measure of the static feel of a golf club. The relationship between the two, if you look at a set of irons, is that - for a set of clubs that are MOI matched - the swingweights of the clubs will increase as you move from longer to shorter irons.

There is a lot of evidence that, for many players, MOI matched clubs play better than swingweight matched clubs. In the last 2 years I have built about 20 sets of clubs using MOI matching, and 1 person said he did not like the feel of them (I rebuilt this set to constant swingweights).

Usually the right MOI for a player's driver is different than that for fairway woods, and the MOI for a set of irons also differs from the woods. MOI matched irons have a similar dynamic weight feel throughout the set. What is typically done in a fitting, say for irons, is to find the best MOI based on testing with say a 6 iron, and then build the irons to that MOI throughout the set. Sometimes, a difference in head weight of as little as 2 grams makes a significant difference in club performance and feel.

MOI club matching is probably something you will hear more of in the future. While not likely to be available in OEM golf stores, it is an option that is available from most true custom clubfitters, and worth considering.

The True Custom Club Fitting
EXPERIENCE – Expectations…

Anyone being "fit" for a set of golf clubs should, I believe, have some expectations on what a superior clubfitting experience will include. Here are some of the things that I believe you should anticipate would happen if you are being truly fit for golf clubs….

> The fitter will first ask you to provide some profiling information about your clubs and your game – which clubs you hit well, which you do not, what are the areas of your game where you would hope to achieve the most improvement.

> You will be asked if you have any physical issues – back, wrist, etc. – that could have an influence on how you swing a golf club.

> The fitter will ask you specifically about what you hope will be accomplished during the fitting. He will tell you what his fitting process is, and what he will need you to do during the fitting.

> The fitter will collect some data on some of your key golf clubs – particularly the ones that are not performing well for you. Length, swingweight,

MOI, flex, loft and lie and face angle for wood clubs at a minimum. It is important to know where you are starting from to help you get where you want to go.

The fitter will know as much as possible about how golf clubs perform and how the 21 Key Variables of Club Fitting affect club performance.

The fitter will take video of your swing as part of the fitting process, and do a thorough review of this video as an initial part of a fitting. The fitter will have enough knowledge of the golf swing to identify any easily fixed swing issues. In some cases the fitter may even suggest that it would be better for the player to take some lessons from a PGA professional before a truly effective fitting can be completed.

The fitter will have an ongoing dialogue with you during the fitting. He will let you see results of measurements made, and let you know when possible improvements are being produced with different fitting clubs. He will also listen to you A Lot during the fitting – what clubs feel good, which are too heavy or light – your input is a key part of a truly successful fitting.

The fitter will let you know the final specifications for the clubs that are being suggested to be built. He will be sure you agree with the results from the fitting. In some cases, particularly iron fittings, it may be necessary to build one or more test clubs for you to use before the final club specs are completed.

When you get your golf clubs, he will ask you for feedback on the performance of the clubs. If they are not performing as you desire, he will modify them as necessary to get the results that you expect.

A few months after you have started playing the fitted clubs, the fitter will ask you for additional feedback on how they are performing. Again, if there are any necessary modifications to the clubs needed, he will work with you to ensure that they play to your expectations.

There is in fact a lot that goes into a True Club Fitting Experience. Throughout the entire process, you also deserve to work with someone who will be as excited about your golf improvement as you will be when you are playing clubs that really fit YOU!!

Is EVERYONE a Custom Club Fitter?

I participated in a very spirited discussion on LinkedIn related to custom club fitting. It was asserted that custom club fitting may not produce the kinds of performance results that golfers expect can be achieved.

There was a lot of confusion in the LinkedIn discussion related to what a Custom Club Fitting actual is. It is best to always go back to the master for such things – Tom Wishon, in the book "The Search for the Perfect Golf Club." Anyone who is interested in the value of true custom clubfitting should read this book. In the book he discusses 5 Levels of Custom Club Fitting, these levels are described in brief below:

LEVEL 1 - The most basic approach. A golfer hits some shots with a limited number of test clubs and test shafts, or may answer a questionnaire on a club company's web site. Simple fitting cart approach. No swing speed measurements. Lie angle of clubs may be tested and fitted. No guarantee on club performance. Falls well short of Level 2 and Level 3 fitting.

LEVEL 2 - Level 1 with use of a Launch Monitor. Limited options for driver face angles, lofts of fairway woods, test shafts. Not as extensive as Level 3.

LEVEL 3 - Includes an interview with the golfer to understand present shot tendencies and desires for improvement. Measuring golfer swing speed with the driver and with an iron (typically a 5 iron or 6 iron). Selecting shaft candidates from a group of many test shafts with varied weight, flex, and flex profile. Building a single pilot test club for irons that can be tested before building the complete set. Fitting process may take 3 hours, sometimes multiple visits.

LEVEL 4 - Everything in Level 3 plus detailed analysis of the golfer's present set and a careful analysis and building of the new set as it is being built. Matching shaft frequencies and club MOIs for irons, identifying the right club MOI, club length, shaft flex profile for drivers. Identifying driver launch angle and spin characteristics that can optimize driver distance. While Tom Wishon did not discuss this in the book, the present versions of Launch Monitors like the Flightscope and Trackman provide extensive information that can make Level 4 fittings result in optimum driver and iron performance.

LEVEL 5 - Level 4 fitting plus for the Touring Pro. This can include grinding of irons to exacting performance specifications. It also includes modifying the look and performance of each iron to the desires of the pro.

If you are hoping to get a "custom club fitting" from a Level 1 or 2 fitting – good luck. Perhaps by chance you may get clubs that are optimized for your game, but it is not likely. True Custom Club Fitting is at the 3, 4, or 5 Level. At these levels you should expect improved performance and lower scores from your clubs – and most likely you will get it!

After I wrote "Is EVERYONE a Custom Club Fitter?", I emailed Tom Wishon, owner of Tom Wishon Golf, about the blog post and asked him his thoughts on updating this. I was excited that he agreed to provide the input on this, as quoted below….

"If I were to re-think this 5 levels of fitting concept, at first thought I would say it would be logical to reduce the number of fittings because 5 seems too many and would challenge a regular golfer's attention span.

But if you want to include a Payne Stewart "design the whole set from scratch so it is a one of a kind" fitting as the ultimate top end #5 fitting, and then if you want #1 to be an OEM fitting or adjustable club fitting, then I suppose you would have to allow for 2 fitting types to be in between. So the total might get down to 4.

Level 1 Fitting. The fittings offered by any pro shop or retail golf store in which only a couple of the 13 key fitting specs are included and each one only for a limited range in fitting options – and this would be only for one or a handful of the clubs in the set, not for all 14 clubs. An adjustable driver with the adjustable hosel piece that only offers a +/- 1.5* change in the lie and face angle + a selection of R or S within one shaft model. This might be considered to be better than no fitting at all where the clubs are strictly bought off the rack, but in no way does it constitute a fitting for maximum game improvement. Not even close. AKA the "phantom fitting" as I would call it – you think you got fit but it was chiefly smoke and mirrors.

Level 2 Fitting. The golfer answers a series of questions about his swing and how he plays. No one actually sees the golfer swing and does not actually see him hit balls to assess his fitting requirements. But if there are enough questions to get proper swing and game improvement needs assessed, and if the clubfitter has a good deal of experience, this is a far better fitting than #1. The goal of a level 2 fitting is still to customize all 13 fitting specs for each of the 13 woods and irons and wedges, but it falls a little short of a Level 3 fitting because the fitter is not working face to face with the golfer.

Level 3 Fitting. The golfer goes to the clubfitter's hitting studio to go through a full swing analysis and face to face interview to assess the golfer's fitting requirements and game improvement needs. Launch monitor is used for sure, previous club specs are measured and analyzed as cause and effect for the golfer's game improvement problems. The golfer hits various test clubs offered by the clubfitter on the basis of the fitter's analysis of the golfer. All 13 key fitting specs for each one of the 13 woods, irons, wedges is custom fit and custom built for the golfer. Usually takes at least two separate fitting sessions – one to analyze and do test club hitting to obtain feedback, then a second one to finalize the fitting specs.

Level 4 Fitting. The tour pro fitting in which the Level 3 fitting analysis determines each of the player's 13 key fitting specs for every one of the clubs, but in addition, each clubhead is specifically designed from scratch for the player's wants and needs. This is a fitting that only a STAR tour player, not even a regular tour player, can get from a golf company that is paying him/her 6 figures and higher to endorse their products.

That's kinda where I am at on this - TOM"

Thank you Tom for updating this, your thinking as always is sound. Hopefully it gives golfers an idea of what does and does not constitute a real custom club fitting.

(Information is courtesy of and copyrighted by Tom Wishon Golf Technology, www.wishongolf.com.)

Custom Driver Fitting 101

Driver Fitting Basics

There is presently a lot of buzz about some new driver heads that have weights about 25 grams or so lighter than present "conventional" driver heads. These are being promoted to produce more clubhead speed and more distance with the driver. One of the ads I saw for a light driver suggested it would be best to play with a 47-½ inch shaft. This is more than 1-½ inches longer than present driver shafts that you can purchase in stores.

I am not convinced that lightweight drivers are a good option for most players. Here are some basics that you might want to consider when you purchase your next driver – hopefully from a precision clubfitter:

> The key fitting elements that affect the performance of a driver are the club length, shaft flex and flex profile, club swingweight or club Moment of Inertia (MOI), club loft, club face angle – AND how you swing the driver (more on that later).

The average length of drivers played on the PGA tour is 44-1/2 inches long. Why? – because this is the length that the best players in the world can hit the best. Most drivers that golfers purchase in golf stores, however, at least 45-1/2 inches long and sometime longer. Why? – because of the constant quest for more distance. Which length do you believe is most likely to give you the best performance with your driver?

For any player of any level of skill, the maximum performance you will get from a driver in terms of Carry Distance is 2.5 times your swing speed. So if you have a swing speed of 100 mph, the maximum carry you will achieve will be 250 yards. No matter what anyone tells you, with whatever head and shaft combination you use, you will not carry the ball further than this. And this is with perfect contact on the sweet spot of the clubhead.

For players with swing speeds of 70 mph or lower, the 2.5 factor is more like 2.2. So for a player with a 70 mph swing speed, the most he will be able to carry his drives is about 154 yards. Again, with best contact on the sweet spot.

Contact with the sweet spot of the driver is king (and queen)! So if you can find a club length, shaft, and swingweight/MOI combination that promotes the most consistent contact on the sweet spot, you will have the best opportunity to maximize carry distance.

For slower swing speeds, drivers with higher lofts can help you to create maximum carry distance. Not everyone plays best with a 9.5 degree loft driver!

Total driving distance – carry plus roll out - is influenced by ball speed, launch angle, and ball spin. The shaft can have some influence on ball spin, but most likely your technique will have a major influence on your ball spin. The ball you play with can also have an influence.

If you decide to have a fitting done for your driver, a key parameter that is measured as part of the fitting is the Power Transfer Ratio – PTR – which is the ratio of the ball speed divided by your swing speed. For drivers optimal PTR is about 1.48 to 1.50, and if your measured PTR is much below this you are not achieving optimum conditions with the driver you are testing.

Finally, if you do decide to hit some very long drivers with lengths in the range of 47-1/2 inches, if at all possible do some tests with impact labels. If you see you are consistently hitting this driver in the center of the face great. But if not most likely this club is too long for you.

Happy driving!

What You Deserve from Launch Monitors: The Basics

The level of technology available to help golfers identify the right golf clubs for them simply keeps getting better and better. There is a range of sophistication of Launch Monitors that are being used successfully today. There are many great launch monitors that can be used to perform custom club fittings - some of the better ones available include the Flightscope, TrackMan, and Vector.

Many of you will either take the opportunity to get a custom fitting where a launch monitor is used, or to participate in a Club Demo Day where a launch monitor is available. Here are some things you should expect to see in terms of the kinds of information that a good launch monitor can provide.

What do Launch Monitors Measure?

Some of the basic data that you should expect to see when you have access to a Launch Monitor include:

- Swing and ball speed
- Launch angle
- Ball spin
- Shot carry distance and total distance

- Club path and club face angle at impact
- Shot path (for example, straight, starts left and curves right, etc.)

A key piece of additional information that can be obtained from the above data is Power Transfer Ratio - PTR – which is:

$$PTR = (ball\ speed\ /\ swing\ speed)$$

PTR is a measure of how effectively your golf club and swing transfer energy from your club to the golf ball. For example, the maximum PTR that can, in most cases, be obtained with drivers is about 1.48 to 1.50.

These data alone are lots of goodies! And appropriate interpretation of this information can help you find clubs that can provide MEASURED improved performance for you.

What SHOULD Launch Monitor data do for YOU?

The kinds of results you should expect to see if you have a fitting based on Launch Monitor data, or if you are viewing this kind of data at a Demo Day, are these:

First of all, does the Launch Monitor actually calculate your shot distances and ball flight? If you know your typical 6 iron travels 150 yards when you hit it well, the Launch Monitor should show carry results of about 150 yards. Same with shot dispersion - if you hit left to right shots the data should show you are hitting left to right shots.

Another "self calibration" that you can do relates to - again using drivers as an example - the predicted driver carry distance for your swing speed. The maximum driver carry distance you can achieve is about 2.5 times your swing speed - so no matter what you do, if you swing at 100 mph you will carry your drives no more than 250 yards. Launch monitor data should be consistent with this maximum.

When you are sure you are getting meaningful data, then the fun can begin. When comparing drivers for example, you can see if a combination of a driver head and shaft can lead to launch angle, ball spin, and PTR data that could result in longer driving distance. Similar things can be done with different combinations of iron shafts and heads - finding combinations that produce more distance, or in some cases for example finding combinations that produce lower or higher ball flight and/or lower or higher ball spin as might be desired.

Launch monitors are great tools (in the right hands!) to truly help you find the golf clubs that can give you the best results.

What Is YOUR Driver Loft?

I think that everyone who buys a driver through the internet deserves to be sure they are getting what they think they are getting. I had some experiences recently with clients that made me want to share some simple information with you about drivers.

If you buy a driver from a web service provider and the advertisement says that it is "10.5 degrees of loft" can you be SURE that is the loft of the driver?

Well…………maybe………….sort of. Here is information that you should really know about buying a driver sight unseen!

> There are two things that determine the True Loft of a driver AS YOU PLAY IT….The real measured loft of the face, and the FACE ANGLE of the driver.
>
> I and other club fitters have measured the lofts of many OEM drivers, and often the lofts are 1 or even 2 degrees different than the number on the club! So if you are hitting your driver higher or lower than you expect, be sure to get your driver loft measured.

Until fairly recently, most drivers I have seen in golf stores have some amount of Closed Face Angle to them. This means that when you set the driver so the face is flat on the ground and you do not attempt to manipulate it so that the face is square to the target line, that the face will look a little shut to the target line. Some players can actually benefit from a closed face angle particularly if the slice the ball. The close face can help them to somewhat reduce the amount of their slice.

However…..if you have a driver that for example has 10 degrees of loft, and say it has a 2 degree closed face angle. Now if you set this driver face so that the face is square to the target line……the EFFECTIVE LOFT of the driver face will actually be 12 degrees. And you might wonder why you hit that driver higher than you think you should.

And the opposite holds true. If you have a driver with 10 degrees of loft and 2 degrees open face angle, and you square the face, then the Effective Loft of that driver will be 8 degrees.

Here is a tip then, particularly if you want to play with a driver that has a face that is square to the target line at address. Make sure you know what you are buying before you click "Purchase." If you want a 10 degree driver with 0 degree face angle, be sure that is what you are buying!

Driver and Fairway Wood Shaft Weight:
A MAJOR Club Fitting Parameter

It is interesting how things come together sometimes to help me learn something valuable to help your golf game.

One of the ways that I personally learn more about clubfitting is to test concepts and ideas on myself. I just put a shaft in my driver that is about a 57 gram shaft, and it is one of the best ones I have ever used. Hitting the ball farther than I have in a long time but more importantly in the fairway.

I had been using 76 gram shafts in my fairway woods, with good results. But I thought why not test the lighter shaft in one of my fairway woods – even though many of my fitting friends typically recommend using heavier shafts in fairway woods than in drivers. So I put the 57 gram shaft in my 3 wood and 5 wood – and could not hit these clubs At All! Back went the 76 gram shafts into these….

Then, this past weekend, I did a Driver Fitting with a player. We started testing with 65 gram driver shafts, and with these his Club Path was about 10 to 12 degrees to the left. So then we tested with 80 gram driver shafts, and his path improved to somewhere between 4 and 8 degrees left. We finally did some testing with a 105 gram steel shaft – and

Amazingly his swing speed went up about 4 mph from earlier results, and path was still better than with 65 gram driver shafts.

What does this mean for YOU? First of all, changing shaft weight has the largest overall influence on the total weight of a golf club (assuming head weight is constant). There are companies selling shafts that weigh 50 and even 40 grams, promoting that these might result in higher swing speeds for players. I know that there are a number of players on the PGA tour playing 75, 85, even 100 gram weight shafts – but so far have heard of few playing very light weight shafts. I believe there are two major things you need to remember related to shaft weight for drivers and fairway woods:

Lighter Weight Does NOT NECESSARILY Mean Faster Swing Speed!

Without testing, you have no idea if a lighter shaft will produce more speed. In fact (as noted earlier) heavier weight might produce higher swing speeds. WHY? – there is a shaft weight that is best for a particular player in terms of how they swing the golf club, how they "synchronize" their swings to hit the golf ball well.

Shaft Weight Affects Golf Club Path.

Lighter shafts can promote a more outside-to-inside club path, and heavier shafts can promote a more inside-to-outside club path at impact. Lighter shafts may be exactly what a strong player does Not need if they already have a tendency to swing outside-to-inside.

Increasing swing speed with INCREASING shaft weight? – maybe Yes, maybe No – something that you would not know without Testing!

What is YOUR Driver Face Angle?

The Face Angle of a driver is the direction that the face points when the driver is sitting flat on the ground and the shaft is straight up and down. Face angles can either be open, closed, or square. It is possible to exactly measure the face angle of a driver in a Lie/Loft measurement gauge.

It used to be that most drivers sold in golf stores had closed face angles. For many golfers, this is actually a good thing for two reasons: a) present day 460 cc driver heads are not easy to close at impact, closed face angles can help with this; and b) many golfers slice the ball, and a closed face angle can help reduce the amount of the slice.

However, it seems like I am seeing more and more drivers with open face angles. For someone slicing the ball, this can make a bad situation worse. Why – well if the golfer has an inside to outside swing path, and their face is very open to that path – big slice!! Why there seem to be more open faced drivers on the market is not something I understand. But it is not something that helps the general golfer to play better golf.

One way or another – you deserve to know if your driver has an Open, Closed, or Square Face Angle. If you do not have easy access to a club fitter who would be able to make an exact measurement of this for you, here are some options:

> Set your driver head flat on the ground in front of you and Be Sure that the shaft is pointing straight up and down. You should be able to see if the face is open, closed, or square.

> Look into a mirror and do the same thing as for #1 – again, you should be able to see visually if the face is open, closed, or very close to square (thanks Hoot Gibson, AGCP club fitter!).

Everyone deserves to know what the face angle of their driver is. You may have been playing with an open faced driver for years and never known it – and you if you have a driver with the right face angle for your swing, it will help you to play better golf.

Wedge and Putter Fitting Excellence

Making Your Wedge Bounce Work

The edge on the sole of your wedge that is closest to the grooves is the Leading Edge. The sole edge that is furthest from the face is the Trailing Edge. When a wedge has positive bounce, the Trailing Edge is lower than the Leading Edge when you address the golf ball. Wedge bounce is basically a golf club's resistance to digging into the ground.

The wear pattern on the sole of a wedge can tell you a lot about how that wedge is working for a golfer. I recently saw a wedge that had significant wear all along the sole of the wedge. If the Wedge Bounce is being "activated" correctly – to allow the wedge to "bounce" through turf or through sand – most of the wear on the sole should be very close to the Trailing Edge of the club.

The wedge wear pattern discussed above can come from a wedge that is not suited for the way a particular golfer swings, due to the design of the wedge (probably not enough bounce on it), or a combination of both. Regardless of why this wear happened, the likely result is that this player has to work too hard to hit good sand shots and/or other types of short game shots.

How can YOU tell if the wedges you have in your bag are working well for the way you hit your short game shots? Well, there are two simple evaluations you can do. First, you can look at the bottom of your wedges and see the wear pattern on them – are you "activating" the bounce? Second, you can put a piece of tape on the bottom of your wedge, and hit some wedge shots off of a lie board – you can quickly see where you are making contact on the bottom of your wedges.

Recently I evaluated the clubs of another player who had Negative Bounce on his Gap Wedge – meaning this club will dig into the ground for all golf shots and not bounce out easily – amazing that someone would design a wedge this way – and luckily he no longer carries this wedge in his bag!

Take the time to learn about how your wedges are working for you – and if they are not, You Deserve Better!

Are You REALLY a Picker?

Recently a potential future client met with me, and during our preliminary session told me that he "picks" his wedges. This means that he takes very little if any divots with his wedge shots. He also indicated that he has a difficult time hitting short wedge shots – from 50 yards and in – well.

Many players think that they are "pickers" with their wedges – but it might just be that Their Wedges Are What "Makes" Them Pickers. If you play a wedge that does not have sufficient bounce – like most of them that are typically available to players – your wedges will not bounce correctly off of the ground during your wedge shots. So, what do you do? – you add more and more forward shaft lean so that you can somehow "pick" the ball clean. Sometimes this seems to work – but often it does not. And so you hit thin shots, and then perhaps you adjust, and you hit fat shots, and then back and forth.

There is a solution. First of all, you need to play with wedges that have the right bounce for your wedge swing. Edel Golf has found that most players need at least 10 to 20 degrees of bounce on their wedges. Most likely then, if you are playing a sand wedge that has less than say 14 degrees of bounce, this club will not work well for you for shots off of the turf. And if your lob wedge has only 6 to 8 degrees of bounce – as many available lob wedges do – then you should put that club on eBay and find one also has lots of bounce – definitely in double digits and perhaps at least 20 degrees.

You then need to work on your wedge technique. No more significant forward shaft lean. Allow the bounce on the club to work. Keep your weight on your forward side during your swing so that it is easier to make good contact.

Once you develop the right technique, and also get wedges that have the right amount of bounce for your swing, you will be amazed at how easy those 50 yard and in wedge shots will be.

AND – maybe, just maybe – you will no longer say that you are a "picker!"

Putters – Cut and Beware

The most important club in a golfer's bag is the putter. Getting the right balance and feel in a putter can make all of the difference between being able to sink 3 footers and roll long putts well. And if the putter does not have the right feel and you do not know it, you might think you have poor putting technique when the truth is you have a poorly fitted putter.

But what happens if you find a putter in a store that you like but it is too long for you? Well, you might decide to cut the putter to make it shorter. That sounds like a good idea and you shorten your putter.

But when you do this, you affect the overall weight feel of the putter. You reduce the swingweight of the putter and – unless you compensate for cutting the length – you make the putter feel lighter and have less feel of the putter head.

If you reduce the length of a putter by 1 inch, you need to add about 12 grams of weight to the putter – either lead tape or perhaps putting tungsten powder down the shaft – to compensate for this length change and get the putter head feel that the longer putter had.

So if you need to reduce your putter length, realize that you also need to modify the putter weight so that you keep the right weight feel for the most important club in your bag.

What Makes a Great "Putter?"

My wife and I recently returned from a wonderful 10 day vacation in Ireland. While there I had the chance to play 4 courses, including 2 great links courses. One of my golfing friends during the trip said the following:

"People who putt better like fast greens"

This comment led me to think about a related question – What Makes A Great "Putter"? The reason I put putter in quotes is that the question has two parts – the equipment and the one who is putting.

Seems to me that to be a great Putter you will more often than not do the following:

- Have great speed control on longer putts;
- Make almost all putts 3 feet or less;
- Make a high percentage of 4 to 10 foot putts;
- Are good at reading greens;
- Make "your share" of putts longer than 10 feet; and
- Have the attitude that you are a great putter – even when you miss some.

I am certain that any one has the potential to be a great Putter if they play with a Great Putter (the equipment). Most people have little chance, though, of becoming a great putter because they self-fit themselves. They are not likely to find a putter that TRULY fits them in terms of aim and speed control.

The Kiss Of Death for finding a good putter that has good aim and speed control is to go to a golf store and putt on a putting carpet and hope that this putter will work on the golf course that you most often play at. While you may be "fit" at a very low level for the right putter length and lie angle, you have no idea if you can aim the putter at a target – and when I say Aim I mean Dead On Right On Line Aim – or if this putter has the right overall weight feel for your golf stroke so that you can easily control speed.

When you actually are fit for a putter that has Great Aim and Great Speed Control, you free yourself up to be able to make a stroke that has few manipulations – you can use your natural stroke to get the ball in the hole, and know that you are not being held back by your equipment.

EVERYONE has the potential to BE a **Great Putter** if they putt with a Great Putter.

Putter Counterweighting is MAGIC!

One of my golfing friends is a few years older than 70. He is still a pretty good ball striker and is capable of shooting scores in the low 80s or high 70s. He has in the past had issues with his putting rhythm and speed control. On short putts he has had a hard time making a smooth stroke. Recently, I offered to do some testing with him using Putter Counterweighting. We tested with 70, 100, and 130 gram counterweights added to the butt end of his putter. With each adding of weight, his stroke became smoother and more confident. When we added the 130 gram weight, he immediately knew this was the best weight for him. I watched him hit short putts – smooth stroke. He had the same smooth stroke, and good speed control, for longer putts. He is continuing to putt better with this counter-weight in his putter.

Counterweighting is adding weight to the butt end of a golf club. It can help improve driver performance and also performance of irons. But in my opinion where it is the most valuable is in putters. Keith Chatham – an AGCP Master Club Fitter - has said his experience is that 80 to 90 percent of golfers putt better with counterweights in their putters.

Counterweight in putters helps the golfer to get more feeling in their hands during the stroke. The right counterweight in a putter helps improve speed control, but perhaps most importantly helps to "smooth out" the putting stroke and makes it easier to hit short putts with more confidence.

About 2 years ago, I worked with a golf club professional who had to putt with a claw grip because he could not control his stroke with a conventional grip. After adding a 50 gram counterweight a few inches down the shaft of his putter, he instinctively changed to a conventional grip because he got the feel back in his putting stroke.

All golfers should test using counterweights in their putters. I expect that the friend who I helped is going to be taking a lot more money from me in the future because he did!

You CAN Achieve Putting Excellence!

October 11, 2012 was an exceptionally satisfying day. We recently purchased a Science and Motion Sports (SAM) PuttLab, the "Cadillac" of putting analysis and putting training systems. Fourteen golfers – including myself – had their putting strokes analyzed by Glen Coombe, "The Putting Doctor," using the SAM. Glen helped each golfer with ways they can improve their putting. Each golfer learned information they never knew about their putting strokes. How does it get any better than that in terms of helping golfers lower their scores!

During the day, Glen said that "Putting is the only area in golf where any golfer can become as good as a PGA professional." Some might argue that, but I think there is a lot of truth in that statement. And since putting accounts for 40% of all golf strokes taken in a round of golf, becoming a great putter can have a huge impact on how well a golfer scores.

So – with that said – what are the appropriate roles of Putter Fitting and Putting Instruction in helping golfers become Great Putters? Is one more important than the other? Certainly the easy answer is that both are important to Putting Excellence. But my thoughts on this are that they need to be "dished out" in the proper sequence and with the proper amount of attention. Here are my present thoughts on the importance of each:

Every golfer who wants to be an Great Putter needs to be taught some key Putting Fundamentals at the start. The proper role of the shoulders and hands in the putting stroke, how to create an appropriate putter path, putting grip, etc.

Then though – and VERY QUICKLY if a golfer wants to become an Excellent Putter – the golfer needs to be Custom Fit for a putter than he can Aim Well and that has the Right Weight Distribution for good Speed Control. This includes a putter that has the right lie angle and length and an appropriate putter loft. Golfers have an AMAZING ability to attempt to compensate for putters they cannot Aim and putters that do not have the right Weighting for them. The sooner they can get a Well Fit Putter into their hands, the better. NO SELF FITTING OF PUTTERS!

Then – once they have a Well Fit Putter and reasonably good Putting Fundamentals, they need to learn what they REALLY do when they are putting. This is the value of a tool like the SAM

PuttLab. It shows you what you do rather than what you THINK you do.

Once you know what you are actually doing in your stroke, you can work with a Putting Coach to develop an Improvement Plan that will take you to a Level of Excellence in Putting. If you can execute this Improvement Plan – with feedback on how you are doing in the process – you can develop a consistent stroke, great aim, great speed control, confidence that you can hit the golf ball where you choose to.

A lot of steps? But MAYBE less effort than continually buying Self Fit Putters, not knowing what you Actually Do When You Putt – and hoping you will putt well!

Make Every Putt!

There has recently been a very active on-line discussion with the title "What is the best tip you would give to help golfers avoid three putting?" This has been on a LinkedIn group – "A Golf & Business Networking Group" – and the thread was started by Roseanna Leaton (thanks!).

There have been something like 100 responses to this initial question, and lots of good thoughts and suggestions. Here are a few things that seem to me to be critical to a golfer developing competence and confidence in his performance when he is faced with long putts. And thanks specifically to Carey Mumford with Clear Key Golf: (http://clearkeygolf.com) for his excellent thoughts on this question...

> First of all, knowledge is important. It is fact that the average initial putt length on the PGA Tour, when the tour player hits the green, is 35 feet. So, us "mere mortals" can expect a longer average distance for our first putts. Also, a number of studies have shown that the optimal distance to hit a golf ball past the hole to give it an opportunity to go in is about a foot. If you hit a putt 5 feet by the hole, it has almost no chance to go in.

Second – have the objective to Make Every Putt, no matter the distance. This is a much more positive and focused thought than thinking to Not 3 Putt. It is also much more productive than thinking "Lag Putt." I was going to title this "Tips to 2 Putt" but in fact even that is a negative thought.

Third – get the right tool in your hand – a custom fit putter that has the right weighting for good Distance Control, and one that you can consistently Aim At Your Target. If you self-fit yourself for a putter, you "could" get it right – but if not you set yourself up to make lots of compensations in your stroke.

Fourth – develop a consistent stroke based on sound putting fundamentals. One that works well for you, that you can reproduce.

Fifth – if you are really serious about being a good putter from longer distances – practice long putts (20 to at least 40 feet) and short putts (2 to 3 feet). With every one of these practice putts, intend to make the putt. Allow yourself to become confident in your ability to control distance and aim well.

Sixth – when you are actually playing golf, adopt a process like Carey has advocated in his writings to allow you to "let go" and to trust that you already know – based on the competence you developed from practice – to perform well with every length of putt.

So – I guess that is more than the "one tip" to not 3 putt – but hopefully all of the pieces are there to help you become a better putter from all distances.

More "You Did Not Know" About Custom Club Fitting

Your First Set of Golf Clubs – The Fit Is STILL IT!

You want to get your first set of golf clubs, and you have read that getting clubs that truly fit you are the best way to go.

But most likely you think – how can that matter for me when I am just starting?

Well, maybe just as much as for players who have well developed golf skills, the right starter set will be well worth the investment. Here are some aspects of a good starter set that can help you:

- A driver that is the right length for you, with enough loft to easily get the ball to carry well in the air;

- A fairway wood with lots of loft that will again be easy to hit and get good carry;

- Perhaps one hybrid club as a substitute for a 4 iron;

- A 5, 7, 9 iron and pitching wedge with "game improvement" characteristics that are forgiving to mishits;

- A sand wedge with sufficient bounce to help you hit sand shots well;

- A putter that is perfectly fit for the right length and lie to make it easy for you to get the golf ball in the hole!

Nine golf clubs – built for you to help you to see good results at the start. And also to help you be able to get good instruction to develop a quality golf swing!

FEEL – A Great 4-Letter Word!

Not every player I build clubs for is greatly sensitive to Club Feel. But almost all are to some extent. I recently did a fitting with a good player who is very sensitive to the feel of the club head. And I am about to start a fitting for a player who I know needs clubs that are a lot longer than normal. For him, feel may be more important that for "standard" length players.

Feel is the Bottom Line of a golf club. I believe that if a club does not feel good in your hands you will never truly hit it well. When I do fittings I am constantly asking how one club feels versus another test club and I weigh highly what players tell me about feel.

What affects club feel? Just about everything! For sure the club Moment of Inertia (MOI) or swingweight are a measure of feel – and these are influenced by head weight, shaft weight, and club length.

I do not think it is easy to quantify what makes one club "feel" better than another – but finding the right feel for a player is one of the most important things that a professional club fitter can do.

FEELING The Clubhead – The Hidden Edge

Almost everyone who I have done a fitting for lately has received some significant benefits from identifying the right weight feel for their clubs. And it does not go one way only – sometimes adding more weight is the key, sometimes reducing weight is what makes the clubs pay better. Some examples include:

- Adding 8 grams of head weight to irons and seeing ball flight trajectory increase significantly.

- Adding just a few grams to a club and seeing impact go from off center to dead in the center of the club.

- Increasing the MOI of a driver and learning that the player can now "feel" the head and control it.

I think all of this makes sense - but perhaps for a less than obvious reason. I believe that, inside of us, we are all attempting as best as possible to hit the golf ball on the center of all of our clubs. And we do the best we can to adjust our swings with the clubs we have to make this happen. But when we get the RIGHT club weight feel, then we allow ourselves to "go on automatic" in terms of hitting the golf ball – center contact becomes effortless, more distance and consistency results.

Bottom line – the right club weighting, sometimes even just a few grams of weight change, can help you shoot lower scores!

Fit The Misses Too!

For every fitting that I do, I ask the player "what are your misses?" The answer to this question often provides initial hints into what kind of club improvements can provide the most value to players.

Many fittings result in increased distance with irons or drivers, or reduced dispersion of shots. But a recent post on the AGCP web site caused me to think there is a lot more to consider in paying LOTS of attention to the Misses players make – maybe more attention to these than to the great shots.

There are a lot of things that can be done to golf clubs to "make misses better." Like fitting with an offset driver when a player slices a lot, or fitting with more loft when a player does not get drives and fairway woods in the air, or even recommending a sand wedge with a very wide sole to make sand shots easier.

So finding ways to increase distance with irons and woods is a great thing to strive for. But just as important is to make sure that the clubs really fit the player's swings – and maybe the best way to helping a lot of folks get more enjoyment in golf is simply to help them make all of their misses better.

WATCHING AND ASKING
Very Important Fitting Tools!

It is important to have things like launch monitors and precise fitting clubs to use in club fitting. But it is JUST as important to pay attention to the way a player hits the ball, and particularly if there are any physical issues that he/she has.

A great case of this happened in a driver fitting that I recently did. At the start of the fitting, when I was about to take some video of his swing to measure tempo and club release point, I noticed that he had a tendency to keep the clubface open at impact. At the time did not know if this was related to swing mechanics or something else, but I "filed it away" for later evaluation.

I asked what his normal "misses" have been with his driver, and he said he missed to the right (push fade). Launch monitor and Golftek data confirmed that this was also true during the fitting session.

One of the driver head options that can help reduce the severity of push-slice misses is an offset-head driver. This head includes both offset and a closed club face, and for players who are not afraid to let the club "play" as it is designed – looking at the clubface closed at address – this can be a great option.

During the process of testing different driver heads, the player noted that he has arthritis in his wrist and this keeps him from easily releasing the club. After hearing that, it became clear that the offset head would be a great option for him. Golftek results showed that the face at impact was close to square and final outside testing showed that he hit this club very straight. 44 inches, 15 degrees true loft, and the offset head. A winner!

Knowing about physical issues is just as important as any other fitting measurement. This fitting was a great reminder!!

There are Grips and There are Grips

A good practice in terms of maintaining your golf clubs is to get them regripped at least once a year. And most often folks do this during the winter months, when they when they do not get to play as often because of cold weather.

When someone talks about "standard size grips" the actual standard is to measure the circumference of the grip 2 inches from the end of the golf shaft and 5 inches from the end of the shaft. Standard at 2 inches is 0.900 inches and standard at 5 inches is 0.807 inches. Then other sizes are based on being below or above these standards.

There are a lot of variables that are worth considering when you get your clubs regripped. One of the often overlooked ones is the size of the grip, particularly if you have problems with your hands and wrists. There are a lot of quality grips available in sizes 1/16th of an inch over up to 1/8th of an inch over standard. These can be a great option when you have issues with your hands. Most often these grips are from 10 to 30 grams heavier than standard size grips. Using these will decrease the overall swingweight of the club and so you may "feel" the clubhead a bit less.

There are now grips in standard size and oversize that are significantly lighter than a typical 50 gram grip. These lighter grips significantly decrease the overall weight of a club, and also increase the club swingweight – you may "feel' the clubhead more with these lighter grips.

Another great option in terms of gripping clubs is to add more tape on the shaft at the lower end of the grip. This will make the club a bit larger in the lower hand, and a lot of players like this feel particularly again if they have hand and wrist problems.

It is worth it, then, to consider all of the potential options that are available to you when you get your clubs re-gripped. You may not know that there is more to this than simply putting a grip on!

AGCP Roundtable – Your Golf Clubs and Your Swing!

I had a great week at the 2011 annual Association of Golf Clubfitting Professionals (AGCP) Roundtable. In fact, it turned out to be the best of the four Roundtables I have attended thus far. Excellent presentations on club fitting, the relationship of fitting and the golf swing, golf fitness and the golf swing, and marketing and business management guidance for clubfitters.

It would be hard to pick out one presentation that was better than others. But it was not hard to remember one of the important overall points from the Roundtable. This point was made by Eric Hogge, the Head Professional at the PGA Teaching and Learning Center in Port Saint Lucie, Florida. Eric said the following....

YOUR GOLF CLUBS WILL TEACH YOU HOW TO SWING

There is definitely a strong relationship between custom club fitting and the golf swing. If you want to develop a good golf swing, and your clubs are too long/short, too heavy/light, etc. your swing will be influenced by your clubs. It also goes the other way – if you have a poor golf swing it is going to be difficult to fit you for a set of clubs that will give you excellent results.

What is important is to strike the right balance in connecting fitting and golf swing instruction. It was great that we spent more than a day of our time during the Roundtable discussing just how to reach this balance to help golfers achieve better results.

Club Fitting – "BEST" to the 4th Power (+1!)

AGCP members are very fortunate to be able to learn from the best club fitters in the world. One of them is Keith Chatham – AGCP Master Club Fitter - from Kerrville, Texas.

From time to time Keith writes things on the AGCP club fitting forum that are just absolutely Right On. He recently did this, in response to a question related to the connection between fitting and golf instruction.

What he said is that if you do your fitting and provide

BEST ACCURACY

BEST DISTANCE

BEST FEEL

BEST CONSISTENCY

That you cannot go wrong.

This to me is my goal and I believe the goal of all of the true, dedicated custom club fitters that I know.

But what is the "+1?" Well, you could argue I think that if you did the above four things how could you do more. But I think the Extra Goal is Listening To The Customer. Being sure he/she has a voice in the fitting, provides feedback during the entire process, let's you know how the golf clubs play, and also lets you know when appropriate how you can improve. Provide the Best Possible Club Fitting Experience!

Custom Club Fitting – PRECISE not CLOSE

Roy Nix – the Founder of the Association of Golf Clubfitting Professionals (AGCP) and Master AGCP Club Fitter – made this statement in a LinkedIn post that has stuck in my mind. This statement was (probably paraphrasing a little!)......

"Off the rack golf clubs have specifications that are close but not precise, custom club fitters build golf clubs that have specifications that are precise not close."

Here are a number of "Close But Not Precise" golf club specifications that I have run into that can affect how golfers score but also how they can enjoy their games:

> A golfer showed me his present gap wedge – one that he practices with a lot and one that has not been easy for him to hit. It actually had Negative Bounce – so when he would impact the ground it would dig into the ground rather than bouncing off of the turf as a good wedge design should. Pretty hard to overcome that poor club design!

> An excellent junior golfer – about to go to college on a golf scholarship – did a putter fitting with me.

I looked at his present putter, made by a well know putter company – and the grip was not on straight. The flat side of the grip was set up so that he would set the putter face closed to his aim line – unless he adjusted. Small thing?

I recently started rebuilding a set of OEM irons with Aerotech i80 S flex shafts for a golfer. To do so, I had to pull the heads from the present irons. The 4 iron was supposed to be 38-7/8 inches long, it was 39-3/8 inches long. Other irons in the original set were also not at the specifications expected. The question is why? – but at least in this case after the clubs are rebuilt they will have consistent lengths, club MOI weights, and club flexes.

If you want to play your BEST golf, you deserve to play with golf clubs that are in fact Precise Not Close to the specifications you need!

Afterword

The Second Annual Knoxville Social Slam – focused on using social media for marketing – was held in April 2012. One of the speakers was Tom Webster, the Vice President of Strategy for Edison Research. He did not know it, but he talked about the value of Custom Fit Golf Clubs!!

During his entertaining and informative talk, he presented a quote that came from Donald Rumsfeld:

**"There are known knowns.
These are things we know that we know.**

**There are known unknowns. That is to say,
there are things that we know we don't know.**

**But there are also unknown unknowns.
These are things we do not know we do not know."**

My experience has been that many golfers play for years and years and do not know how their custom club fitting can help them improve their golf game. My hope for this book is that you will learn the custom club fitting "unknown unknowns," and can use this knowledge to help you achieve your golfing dreams!

Who Is This Guy?

I was fortunate to have a 35-year career as a scientist and technical program manager at the Oak Ridge National Laboratory (ORNL). In 2006, after that "little voice" told me to do so, I pursued a second career and passion as a professional club fitter. In April 2011 I retired from ORNL and became a full-time professional club fitter.

For the last 4 years, I have been an active participant in the Association of Golf Clubfitting Professionals (AGCP) – the greatest club fitting education organization in the world. The AGCP has a clubfitting certification program, and I am presently a Level-10 Certified Professional Clubfitter.

I use the knowledge I have learned in the past 6 years, the state-of-the-art Flightscope Launch Monitor, an extensive group of test clubs, and interaction with golfers to do custom golf club fitting. I wrote an eBook on the Custom Club Fitting process that I use, this is available on my web site.

I use the highest quality custom golf club components in my fitting efforts. I am a Miura Golf club dealer (the only one in East Tennessee), and also use Tom Wishon Golf, Alpha Golf, and Infiniti Golf club heads. I fit with ACCRA, KBS, Aerotech, Aldila, and SK Fiber shafts.

I also have a HUGE passion for helping golfers improve their short games. I am trained in using the Edel Golf putter and wedge fitting systems, and am the only Edel putter and wedge fitter in East Tennessee. I also use the Science and Motion (SAM) PuttLab to measure the 28 key variables in a putting stroke and to assist me in helping golfers improve their putting. I am the only professional club fitter in Tennessee who uses the SAM PuttLab.

Please drop me a line if you have any questions on the information in this book, if you need some information to help your golf game, or if you just want to talk about club fitting. Again thank you for reading this book, I would love to hear from you!

Tony Wright
Game Improvement Golf
tony@gameimprovementgolf.com
865-384-3753
www.gameimprovementgolf.com

The Fit Is IT!!

More Goodies!

To learn more about Custom Club Fitting and how it can help you play the golf of your dreams, go to: http://www.agcpgolf.com/

To find a Certified AGCP Club Fitter near you, go to: http://www.agcpgolf.com/locator

To obtain more detailed information on Custom Club Fitting, read these books:

"12 Myths That Could Wreck Your Golf Game," by Tom Wishon (November 2009)

"The NEW Search for the Perfect Golf Club," by Tom Wishon (June 2011)

"Commonsense Clubfitting, the Wishon Method," by Tom Wishon (2006)

To read the best books available on Putting Instruction, read:

"GOLF The Best Putting Instruction Book Ever!"
by the editors of Golf Magazine (October 2010)

"There is More to Putting Than Meets the Eye,"
by Lanny Johnson M. D. and Howard Twitty (2012)

"Unconscious Putting: Dave Stockton's Guide to
Unlocking Your Signature Stroke,"
by Dave Stockton and Matthew Rudy (September 2011)

"The Putting Prescription: The Doctor's Proven Method
for a Better Stroke,"
by Craig Farnsworth (May 2009)

To download my free eBook on the Elements of Custom Clubfitting, and to sign up to receive my Monthly Club Fitting Newsletter, go to my web site home page:
www.gameimprovementgolf.com

To sign up to receive my weekly "Club Fact" blog post by email, go to my blog post web page:
www.gameimprovementgolf.com/club-fact-blog

Made in the USA
Lexington, KY
19 March 2016